Listeners at the Breathing Place

Princeton Series of Contemporary Poets
Theodore Weiss, Editorial Adviser

Other Books in the Series

Publication of this book has been aided by a grant from the Paul
Mellon Fund of Princeton University Press
This book has been composed in VIP Aldus

Listeners
at the
Breathing Place

Poems by Gary Miranda

Princeton University Press
Princeton, New Jersey

Acknowledgments

Certain of the poems in this collection have previously appeared in various magazines, as follows:

Arion's Dolphin: "Boy Playing Kick-the-Can"

The Atlantic Monthly: "Arrowhead," "Horse Chestnut"

The Colorado Quarterly: "Going"

Mademoiselle: "The Gardener"

Poetry: "Survivor," "Collision," "Reconnaissance" (under the title "The Thickets of Sleep")

Poetry Northwest: "The Magician," "The Moth-Hand," part two of "The Seed That Dies" (under the title "Lines for an Imaginary Son")

The Southern Review: "Triptych"

Southwest Review: "The Bruiser"

Transpacific: "The One That Got Away"

Yankee: Part one of "The Seed That Dies" (under the title "Birthday Poem for My Daughter")

Parts of the poem "The Small Owl of Complaint" have appeared in other forms and with other titles in the following publications: *Audience, Descant, Shenandoah, Story: Yearbook of Discovery, West Coast Review*, and *Yankee*. The first three stanzas of part five originally appeared in *Poetry as* "The Must-Be-Admired Things." The final three stanzas of part ten originally appeared in *The New Yorker* as "This Choosing."

The translations from Rilke used as divisions between the three sections of this book are by W. D. Snodgrass, A. Poulin, and Babette Deutsch, respectively.

Contents

Part One

Arrowhead

First, you must find a rock
that has always wanted to be
a bird: to sing, fly.
It is hard.

Next, you must chip away
its minor desires, respecters
of ground, moss; the irrelevant
sparks.

You must shape it into the un-
romanticized heart: tongue
for the deep kiss, shoulders
for holding.

Finally,
you must teach it to cover
its tracks. Wind-breaker,
it must learn

to mend the shards of air
as it goes, swift, tender,
to the bone. It is
hard.

Like Snow

Some people would remember iron
railings, the color of buildings,
how a dog circled three times
before settling in—novelists,
certainly, or just good talkers.

Most of us take only the light
from a place, and translate even that
into the way our spirits shape
the light. We flash into knowledge,
which, if we ignore it, will not forgive us.

Objects can survive fine on their own,
but the feel for how this face, that
window, falls upon the momentary
way we hold ourselves could easily
get lost, and who would find it?

Such loss, if lived with, stiffens
into pain; it stands up, starched
and handsome, ready to please the neighbors.
We find ourselves forgetting dreams, whole
days, the last time we were honest;

we ask ourselves: say something
in childhood, and feel only the weight
of what that means brush against
our face like snow. "Like snow,"
we say, not even coming close.

Collision

Moon, stars, an apology of constellations
ride the freeway toward this ample, if
somewhat routine, accident. You lie there,
your life reduced to physics, the laws
of light, the laws of inertia.

You try to remember the acronym
for the rainbow's colors—a man's name.
You know it is not Yves Bonnefoy.
You think of Father Falsetto, who gave you
your only C, in physics. You think

of the time he caught you in the boys' room
dispensing the paper towel roll onto the floor
and gave you a sermon on waste. "Senseless,"
he said, turning, and you stood there
wondering why you had done it: something

about a river, or the way sound
travels. How did they get those voices
into the wires, really? Or, if they did,
how explain portable radios? So many
things to learn. . . . *Roy G.*

Biv! Red, orange, yellow, green. . . .
A state trooper puts his face so close
to yours he looks like a giant bug
in a horror movie. "Blue," you say.
"Indigo," you say. "Violet."

It seems to work. The face is human
now, but you have become the luckless
hero, the only one who has seen the monster
and whom no one will believe. *Save
your breath,* you start to think, then

stop, to think: *Save your breath!*
You wonder if you will ever speak again,
and did you say "violet" or "violent"?
It makes such a difference, unless. . .
unless. . . . They are lifting you up:

through the glare of headlights—or perhaps
the backs of your eyelids—the moon,
the stars, collide in a metaphor
for all you had wanted your life
to be. Violet. Violent.

Boy Playing Kick-the-can

Stock-upright behind the trunk of the oak,
he has grafted himself to the tree, as far
as he's concerned,
and is not concerned with the world behind him
that has no eyes and is no threat.
Like the man who left his wife for a day
and stayed away for twenty years,
our boy's a sure bet for endurance.

The shouts of his playmates
making their bids for the can
and winning or losing
are facts from a different plane
from the one he moves—or, rather,
stands still—on. He has mastered
the art of detachment
and cannot be governed by time's unsubtle tricks.

If the sun goes down, if his mother calls and calls,
he will hug this oak with his shoulder
like Pyramus at the wall:
untroubled, faithful.
This silence sets him apart,
and if he breathes at all
it is only as loud as the sound of the oak tree
growing.

"What the plant is by an act not its own. . .
that must thou make thyself to become,"
as Coleridge says. And he does.
He is taking root as the summer evening noises—
muffled dogbarks, horns from a distant
freeway—float his way like a quiet breeze
and ruffle the leaves of his hair,
but very gently.

The Gardener

Poetry he would hardly have understood,
or countenanced.
Frost, to him, was what killed flowers.
He knew that well enough.
Camellia, mum, sweet William:
he labeled them all with Popsicle sticks
his grandchildren bequeathed.

Out in the garden,
his shoes like moldy loaves of bread,
his overcoat undone,
he strove like any surgeon to preserve.
Goldfish could survive the cold,
locked in their stone sea,
but flowers couldn't.
The breath from his mouth made daisies
in the air;
the real ones died, always.

And so it was
he recognized death when he saw it coming,
blue and clumsy, to claim his lungs.
Even in his dreams you could watch him
digging in against it,
crouching to ward it off:
he would lodge his palms for warmth
against his chest, testing the soil
with the tips of his fingers.

The odds didn't matter.
It had never been a question of outcome.

Ars Poetica

Ambiance, feckless, ineluctable:
sometimes you think it would all be clear
if you merely increased your vocabulary,
learning words that line up possibilities
like birds on a wire, or clothespins.

The real trick is to let the whole
menagerie of undone acts leap toward you
so that your surprise is not an act—or,
if an act, an act of recognition you've
been saving expressly for strangers.

Commas, quarter-moons, kindnesses:
those metal humps on bridges that the car
goes over and you know there is no
cause for alarm. You gather them in
with, almost, love. They take you home.

Elegy: For Twenty-three Young Girls
Drowned off the Island of Crete, 1972

". . . desires fell mutely on the waves and drowned
like lovesick girls for whom the world seems too confined."
—Nikos Kazantzakis
The Odyssey: A Modern Sequel
(Trans. Kimon Friar)

1. The Day

The day began like a casual mistake,
one that, overlooked, could be easily corrected,
as when donkeys crapped on the cobblestones
and the donkeymen wielded their bags and brooms
with nothing approaching alarm.
The sun was the sun from a child's painting:
water-color red, not quite round.
They eyes of the houses and shops
blinked once and then
settled into their usual poses,
anticipating midday.
Shadow-fingers of pine and cypress
pointed toward the sea,
but no one paid attention.

The day overturned with the small skiff overloaded with
    children.
Tangled in the yellow nets
they thrashed like fish, they became fish,
learned the exigencies of water:
twenty-three girls
whose lives became what moments remained,
turned old in the flashing of angles,
strangling in this element stranger than air or fire .
as the boatful of boys approached too slowly
the fish-eyed frozen-open disbelief of the twenty-three
grown one now as a fact, or a scream.

The day became this violent mistake
and the slim vestiges of order gave out:
the fisherman forgot his fee,
the teachers turned from backgammon and retsina,
the priest learned the price of prophecy,
the onlookers loosed their tourniquets of grief.
The children drowned.
And the sea, that vast anomaly,
made shuffling human noises,
like a sea.

2. *The Girl*

I am wise now: I have no desires.
I have become like the water,
a continual sound to others,
who have desires.

But I wanted once so many things:
the boys at school
to see I no longer moved like a child,
the baker not to pinch me so
when I went to his shop for tsoureki.
I wanted to brush and brush my hair
with a violent tenderness
and an understanding between us.
I wanted to watch my breasts grow full and firm
like the breasts of my sister,
the dark centers yearning for something.
I wanted my eyes to startle,
and to hide their own alarm, like a woman's.
So many things.
I wanted to lie down—not in the sea—
and feel the turning of grass in the wind
like a light hand over all my body
moving slowly slowly down my slimness
to the new curve of my hips.
I wanted a lover.

12

There are people who live
who know these things are so much foolishness.
I hear them above me now,
their words mixing like the sound of talk at recess
or the senseless clatter of birds at noon.

But I wanted to learn.
I wanted my own despair.

Going

TO GEORGE SEFERIS

Dying is not the worst you could do, old man.
There are places in the world where rockers sit
for decades on a porch and fade and dry

to a chalky semblance of themselves. You go
like a heron down some swamp, its long wings
taking the air in gulps so that the trees

seem to lean in against their wills and listen.
Listen: the sound of your going has a length
of its own. Years fall from your death like rain.

Digging Through to China

The first shovelful cuts
like a scalpel, turning up
nothing we didn't expect:
the lawn's underside, white
roots, perhaps a dog's bone.

After that the enemy
is monotony, not sweat. Roots
get larger, darker. We glance around
for trees as the shovel's sarcastic
smile slices connections.

A grave, we think, needing this
initial deception. We make it wider
for friends, lovers, our large family.
Wider, remembering children. Our
enemies, damn them, can dig their own.

But now, too deep for graves,
we decide we are building a mound,
not digging at all. We marvel
at how the pile of earth resembles
no hole we know, not even reversed;

we call it a sign, this pointing,
mythologies of our best selves.
Finally, all our devices fail.
We are two selves deep in the dark
mother. Where does the dirt go now,

how do we climb? We knew this would
happen. Night fastens its tight
lid and we nuzzle into the soft
with our noses, whimpering, sniffing
for stars, not China.

Reconnaissance

Dreams
have luminous edges,
like the flash of some object
in a copse of trees

that sets the mind's eye
guessing: eyes? a bird's
beak? wet
leaves? a gun barrel?

The thickets of sleep
are thick with creatures of
anger and love,
against which the beams

of your thought
are useless. They lurk
there, as patient as earth,
and as hungry.

And when at last
they turn on you (as they will),
to expect them not to kill
in the most

effective way they know how
would only be
to insult their sincerity.
Whatever they are,

they know they will never
leave that place alive,
and they do not believe
in limited war.

Listeners at the Breathing Place

*"The seal hunters sometimes call themselves
listeners at the breathing places."*
    —From Eskimo Prints, *by James Houston*

The air says what it means, regardless of what
we want it to say. It holds our breath. Conundrums
tumble like seals. We listen. We catch one,
if we are lucky, the way a camera catches the gallop
of horses, their legs in positions we would never imagine.

Van Gogh knew. There is something to be said
for the word's inadequacies, the swirls of light
and movement which will always escape, astound us.
Rain on water, a lover's turning to go. Those places
breathe too, saying: "Be brave, believe in us."

In the end, we will lay down our words and embrace
the air that shapes them here, just as, at the peak
of loving, a cry shakes the candle's aureola in a room
too small for all this, and the body for now needs
to be held, to be held back, from that blinding other.

Triptych

FOR MARIANNE VONZWECK

1. Icarus

You never hear about my mother, though that sun,
imploding its brilliant exigencies, bore
a striking resemblance, up close. My father
should have warned me—though perhaps I just
wasn't listening or had no experience
to tune my ear to his meaning. I could tell
you about rage, now: archipelagoes of red
detonating in some liquid, but not quite
mixing; aloft on its wings, the mind remarking
even in its terror: Lovely . . . lovely! Perhaps
I fell because I wanted to tell my brother
the sea what it was like up there, or warn him,
in terms he might understand, to escape.

Idling in the blue air, the left wing of my
silence tilted toward home, a nervous
tic I hoped to correct with practice. Wax
might really have worked had that breast
practiced a little self-control, not blazed so
with passion, incestuous. Worn down by the sea,
no sibling of mine as it turns out, these
feathers grow incongruous, hardly suffice
as fins, resemble—if anything—the nubbins
of a three-month fetus. Wiser now, I learn
to use what I have, shuffling toward shore.
Flying is for birds. Given a second
choice, I decide to be born.

2. *Orpheus*

Darkness bloomed, and in that space
which was the shape, still, of the flower,
light declared its name—a sound I knew.
But I knew too the illusion of trust
that touches all we can name by language,
calling the sky "a grey slate" or clouds
"the color of erasure." How much we trust
depends on what's at stake—in my case,
love, I thought, though I was mistaken.
Trees understand the word for "sky,"
but not for "leaf," as if the whole of life
were learning to know the enemy—that is,
the one from whom you need love the most.

The importance of what we want is clear,
however inaccurate. The sound of it
follows us at distances too close
to question, like the sound of a dripping
faucet you hear—listen for, rather—when
the faucet is not dripping: a kind
of silence, spliced; or the way an eye
fixes for a moment a star, any star,
then loses it again. "Gun" will never do
for that object, held to the back of your head.
Call it "history." You will learn to forgive it.
You turn around to face your first love,
Darkness, gone. And you hold your own.

3. Sisyphus

All things are near, imagining. The words
of sages, or even of damn good poets, seem
easy enough once they're out there, shimmering.
If I could, I would lift this stone like a crust
in the wind and wait for the gull of time
to dive, or spin it, light as vowels in the mouths
of infants, who choke on the coarse consonants.
I would strike an armistice with stone, saying:
your metaphors hold, they last—the child
against the radiator its head, the drunk
into the hard bench of winter, heart in the rib
cage, tongue in the teeth. This stone is a moon
against which the wolf of my one life howls.

Courage is not inexhaustible. It gets beaten
down to a fine edge of sadness, like that slice
of horizon crushed between earth and sky.
Or like an old woman who sits and darns,
replacing the essence of socks with the dark
thread of her own death, reducing all clothes
to the negative of clothes. But look: how
she makes the tiny point turn needle again,
the way a god might push a star clear through
from the other side. Such motion precludes meaning,
or else defines it. I have a gift for making truth
irrelevant. Behind my eyes, like a lost shoulder
of the sea, the moon of my next self rises.

Part Two

How many regions in space have been
inside me already. Many winds
are like my son.

—*Rilke*
Sonnets to Orpheus

The Bruiser

FOR MY BROTHER

My sophomore year in high school
we played a lot of basketball together
and once—one game against St. John's—
I tackled ol' Moose Farrell at midcourt
because he elbowed, underneath the board,
you, who didn't believe in anger.

My junior year they took you away
and put you somewhere out of reach,
and no one told me who to tackle then
or even talked about it at all,
because it hurt, yes, and too because
it left a kind of mark, like fingerstains.

Later on they let you out from there:
electric shock had cured you, a kind
of magic in your mind, like lightning.
But still no one would talk about it,
not even you, and memory under our
noonday silence bleached and disappeared.

This alone survives from all that year:
you in the tub one evening as I shaved
and telling me that I should leave
so you could drown yourself,
your eyes unfixed except on fixtures
and empty, like the drain.

And still in dreams I see you drowning—
not in tubs but in rivers under boards—
and wake in sweat because I cannot save you.
And TV shows about the place you went
can valve up tears without my knowing why—
until I think on it, and conjure: you.

I only say: perhaps we should have talked
about it, spread it out across our knees
and talked and talked and talked about it
until it couldn't hurt us any more. For how
was I to know they hadn't killed you there,
you see, and sent me back a new one?

Horse Chestnut

I fell from one once. Judy Cole
used to put five of them, whole,
in her mouth. My brothers ran to tell
my mother: It's Gary—he fell
from a tree but he isn't dead
yet. As I write, there is one outside
my window. I have a weakness, still, for
women with large mouths. The doctor
put two fingers into my head,
tingly with novocaine, and said
to my mother: Look, you can see
where the skull is chipped. Sometimes we
made pipes, or necklaces. My mother
groaned and looked away. I could never
figure out what connection they had
with horses.

Later, Judy Cole was named Miss
Seattle. Mostly, what I remember is
blood all around and me lying
there thinking: so this is dying.
Every one of them has two inside,
like testicles. I wasn't afraid
really, just convinced. By the time I began
to think I loved her we had been
children too long for it to matter.
Sixteen stitches. I saw her once later,
when she was married. My mother
said: I don't want to see you near
that tree again—understand? I still tend
to confuse dying and love. And
no one I've ever loved has died,
exactly.

Some of This Really Happened

To say that there are possibilities for passion
would only undermine that premise, and yet
simply to act on it would hardly communicate.
I would like in these lines to effect a fusion

of statement and act (though statement is winning
at the moment—owing, no doubt, to the obsessive
refusal of words to leap, dance, make love,
or otherwise perform on the page) into meaning.

In the pine forests behind Pac City (when you get
beyond the dunes, which rise like what easterners
would call mountains, only whiter) I discovered
once an explosion of wild rhododendrons—red,

ivory, violet—so startlingly out of place
in that dominance of sky-blue, pine-green, that I
became at first afraid—the way you do under the sea,
accosted by beauty so strange you can barely face

it. It made me think—accused me almost—of the times
I used to shinny up the clothesline crossbar behind
Judy Cole's house, knowing how the warm throb in the
    groin
would shudder the whole length of my legs as I climbed.

And turning my eyes away when I finally could, I saw,
off Cape Kiwanda, the heartbreakingly helpless body
of my brother slip like a white petal from the jetty
of rock and fall, soundless, to the breakers below.

The Magician

FOR AN UNCLE, DROWNED AT SEA

I remember you at the bathroom mirror
practicing sleight-of-hand,
trying to master all the angles
like a guilty husband.

Or I think of the time you nearly drowned
at Wilderness. My father
pumped your chest long past necessity
and a crowd gathered

and I was sure your breath was a toy
no tears could buy.
But you came back, a regular
Houdini.

By now you are an accepted fact,
even to the fish. Dead,
you are as unastonishing
as love that has outworn its need.

It will do no good to toss in your sleep,
accumulating patter.
Because, uncle, there is no crowd
and it does not matter

that death has taught you to hold your breath
for years at a turn.
It is a trick
anyone can learn.

Mt. Auburn Cemetery, Cambridge

Money bought these graves.
It makes me think of my
grandfather dead in Seattle
and the letter they sent his
wife, explaining: if we don't
receive your check by return
mail we will be forced to remove
the marker.

White petals drop from a rhododendron
bush. On the pond a duck and drake
refuse to leave each other's side
although the pond is so small
a mayfly measures it off over
and over before the petals
even have time to drift
to the bank.

I did not see that letter,
I only saw my grandmother's
face as she told me how she hated
to ask for money and how those men
were not bad men but merely
doing their jobs, her face
not angry but white and
very small.

I do not know what kind of ducks
these are or if, in fact,
the mayfly is a mayfly, but
I know that is a rhododendron
bush because it is the state flower
of Washington and also because
even the bushes here
have markers.

Amtrak

Corridors keep shaking where I move,
and in those corridors faces that are not
paintings. There must be something no one
understands which will explain all this.

A pretty woman with a face that doesn't
let go easily runs her fingers through her hair
and shakes her head at no one. This happens
on a train from Boston to New York and back

again, day after day, where she is the hostess
in the cafe car—day after day, except that today
I am here to see this gesture which I know
defines her private grief. She thinks there must

be more to what she wants than riding Amtrak
back and forth and shakes her head to say so,
strokes her hair. And if she were not pretty—
or if, that is, her hair did not remind me of

another woman's hair—I would not even notice
what I notice, which is sad. Even if she
noticed me, I know I could not make her happy—
not day after day—any more than this train

can, which is sad. If you find bones someday—
in a field just starting to get the hang
of wildflowers—bones that strafe the sky
in every direction but the one that matters,

they are hers. Meanwhile, America passes by
like a man other men know, easy in bars, easy
with one kind of woman. She leans too far
into that man's need for something different

from anything she knows; calls it her life.
Me, I'm lucky: I have a friend in New York,
a friend in Boston, a ticket on this train,
this poem, and more memories than I'll ever need.

Survivor

FOR CONRAD CASARJIAN

If that was God, he was neither large
nor particularly interested. He winked
at me, as though this were a joke, this
dying. I have seen him more clearly
in the groan at the far edge of love,
caught in his hands like a child, falling.

The river was not a bathtub, this
was not a joke. Everything slowed down
as in those movies at school where buds
burst to flowers in a second—like those
movies, but run in slow-motion—that is,
normal—but not, for those movies, normal.

It is a hard thing to explain, but
somehow the river seemed to be stuck,
like a record moving at its usual speed
and nothing happening except the same
sound over and over. I was the needle,
waiting for someone to come and fix me.

How long would it take them to notice!
I am trying to tell you this as calmly
as possible: it was not the water, it was
the air, betraying me, turning into a
monster as I watched. I knew it was
useless to try and change its mind.

The shore sat there—sad, but not very—
the trees shaking their heads a little,
helpless. Nothing was violent, only
strange. The clouds—there were clouds—
made faces I did not understand, like
God's. No one was on my side. Yet

I am here. You notice. A little less
interesting than someone who really drowned.
Whatever intervened loved me, I think.
Not God, not the river. More the child
inside, remembering, deciding to put its
small strengths into one place, like coins.

The One That Got Away

Man, you got a bird where your brain
should be, he says, talking to me.
I say: Perhaps you'd like to explain
that figure of speech for the whole class.

He says: A bird, man, a bird—thass
one o' them things with wings what flies
around. You, you jes sits on your ass,
but your brain it flies around, goes

flap an' flap—like this. He shows
me then with his arms, doing flap-an-flaps
between the aisles like a trained crow's
bad imitation of a little black

boy flying. Then he flaps to the back
of the room and out the door, free:
free of the class, that doesn't crack
a smile; free of the teacher, who sits

on his ass, a bird where his brain should be.

The Seed That Dies

We are the seed that dies. And I entered my empty house.
—George Seferis

1. Daughter

Child,
your birthday comes around:
we've been here before.
I've written so many poems to you in my mind,
you go anthology on me.
One would almost think you were real.

They told me, once, you were there, you *were* real,
in the soft of her womb, waiting,
becoming something—and then deciding against it.
Nobody's fool, I played, just the same,
small games of belief
and rehearsed and rehearsed and rehearsed your names.

Over the years how they've changed—
Lisa, Julie, Jennifer, Ann—
the last a name you take from your mother, whom you
     resemble
except for the eyes, which are mine
(though they dart, as you fall asleep in my lap
sometimes, under the lids, like hers).

Over and over I introduce the world to you
and you to the world,
as if I were practicing Greek:
Na sas sistíso—who?
We've got to decide on that.
We've got to quit playing, girl, and get down to life.

I light your life like a candle, year after year,
and you, like a child, make a career
of blowing it out. Games . . . games.
I love you, my moveable feast, but oh my first- my un-
born. . . . Child,
I am dying.

2. *Son*

Today you occurred, perhaps for the first time,
were born announcing how I've neglected you
all these years, steeped in mythologies of daughters.
What did you do, you say, not to deserve even
gratuitous love? And I grope (let's say you are five)
for answers, as though you had just asked me
about sex (which you have) and wonder what the hell
your mother (which you haven't) would say. I say:
Let's go for a walk.

Outside, the October trees are a raised chorus, small
leaves rehearsing their litany of let go. I think
to you: Listen to trees! I say: Are you warm enough?
I know: soon my answers will have to turn stark
as these trees. I try to remember what it was like
being a boy and wish, in a weak moment, you might
have grown up like me, afraid or perhaps too proud
to ask anything, a briar-root spiralling into itself.
I tell you a story:

I had a cousin once, older than me, who had a dog,
a collie, that could find us playing hide-and-seek
no matter where we hid, that dog smarter than any kid
in the neighborhood. The cousin got killed in the war
(except I know that isn't right because he wouldn't

38

be old enough, but still . . .) they shot him down
in the cold Atlantic and no one ever found the body (this
is true) and I kept thinking: the dog, send the dog!
(Or was it my father?)

I shout then: *Look, I don't want a son, how would I know
how to make you love me?* You are hurt. I want
to make myself not to have said that, or explain, or say:
Now that I've said it everything will be all right.
But you have already let go of my hand and are walking
away toward the grey mouth at the end of this clutch
of trees. I watch you go, wondering will you be warm
enough, and why in hell did you buy that cap if you never
put the flaps down?

The Moth-hand

Bruised and white,
the moth-hand flutters toward the light-
switch, transparent as gauze.
Immune to my critical eye, it has no shame,
is what it is,
seems to have no memory of what it was.
I cannot say the same.

I cannot believe
that the hand can gather its strength to move
after all it's been through.
I watch it as one would watch
a crippled war hero stripping in public,
trying pathetically to recapture attention
the only way he knows how.

I think of the hand's women,
of its features memorized line by line,
its fingers lingering along the lips
of a mouth half open, half closed,
or entering the soft chambers of love.
I remember when its every movement seemed
quick or angry or emphatic or furtive.

Now we are like lovers
who have quarreled—not once but over and over
until the issue is impossible to distinguish.
I try to think what it might mean.
But the light clicks off, and the moth-hand
glows for a long moment,
sizzling in its one wish.

40

Second-born Son

LINES FOR WALT WHITMAN
COMPOSED ON NANTUCKET ISLAND

1.

This house, September, and a woman
even you could believe in. I came here
on a ferry to write these lines about you, I
in my thirty-sixth year in perfect health,
as you would say, as you did say, and I too
a second-born son enamored of ferries:
the continuous white froth behind, the sea-birds
gliding impossibly close to water or diving
for scraps as you did into your chaos,
content with what scraps you could find there.
Sideswiped by any grace, how the faces
of strangers undid you, Tuesday through Monday—
cab drivers, ferrymen, widows—that world
you owned like a lamp you could not stop
rubbing. But especially on ferries,
wide-mouthed and handsome: who worried
about destinations? And the sun and moon
on opposite horizons falling and rising
as though connected by wires, the sun orange
and the moon orange. And you between sea floor
and sky floor, your reflection pendant, a creature
alike of air as of water, the face that you loved
there wistful and whiskered and your hat cocked
as you pleased, and your slow omnivorous smile.

2.

The light here could take you like touch
away. Goldenrod. Bird Flash. Shadow.
But this wind—howl-sick, unsettling—listen:
whistle in the underpinnings, window-caresser.
Houses you built with your brothers in Brooklyn,
a trade learned from your father who, even as you
whistled down your reckonings toward tomorrow,
lay there dying of what he missed, some lack
you tried hard to supply with your words—
supple, insinuating, carefree, careening toward
disasters you had not begun, luckily, to understand.
Between the soles of your feet and that hard
earth what a sad distance. Earth and father
you coupled, saving for mothers the sea,
or the moon—sagging, yellow-breasted, brown-
nippled—oh how you courted it, eclipsing
with your father's house-building hands
its uncentering brilliance at the last minute.
Hammerblow and firedamp. So far down
no wind would howl there but only the dark
interstices of your firstlove floating you back
to such omnipotence as you could muster.
All your moons are mothers, and the womb,
given its own good time, has its own revenge.

3.

Which self was it, Walt, that called you
to the window that dusk as your father
lay dying, your only older brother going mad,
your youngest brother crippled and half-witted,
your mother knitting her yarn of helplessness
around you all tighter and tighter—to that window
where you saw prefigured in clouds off Long Island
your own face and heard the late mockingbird
speak your name in the elms? I see you there
tentative as the first stars, turning not bright
but transparent as glass through which you wander
into the evening to become the lover of lonely
housewives, the begetter of invisible children,
sounder of depths, food for the hungry
who do not know they are hungry, salt
for their food and their wounds, flesh-fiber
and muscle-fiber, mica on the rock, dust mote
in the day-ending light that streams past your body
and shapes on the silent form of your father
the elongated shadow of his second-born,
looming like nightfall. And in the manuscript
the long dusty avenues of your lines rise
weightlessly from the page and wind off toward
some zero of expectation, high over Paumanok.

Part Three

You, neighbor God, if sometimes in the night
I rouse you with loud knocking, I do so
only because I seldom hear you breathe
and know: you are alone.

—*Rilke*
The Book of Hours

The Small Owl of Complaint

FOR RON, TERRY, RICK, AND PAT MIRANDA

*I love him who chastises his God because he loves
his God: for he must perish by the anger of his God.*
                                        —*Nietzsche*

*Consider the barnstorm flight
of the owl out over fields
and copse, its wingtips
skimming the tops of the round
trees, its talons hinged and ready
as any thought you can think of.*

Think of

*the soft fur of the field mouse,
ruffled by shadows of winds,
its insides churned to nervous
twitchings at leaves that have gone
unfriendly, facts that only
its bones can understand.*

Understand

*that none of this matters, that owl
and mouse are intricate beads
some stranger fingers whose mind
is a moon rising elsewhere, a round
O, a small mouth in the night,
in any night, wherever you go.*

1.

Fields.

Not waving fields, but thistle-thick grasshopper patches
where walking was a literal *tour de force*
and ground made you know you'd been there—
fields that answered the wilderness within,
said Yes to a private terror
a city kid could cherish.
I could shape a savannah around such places.

Jar in hand, holes poked in the lid,
I'd approach a grasshopper knowing he jumped
and spat, and no one around to help.
Spikes on his hind legs and eyes like portable mothers,
that missed nothing, he knew what I knew—
that timing, not size, made the difference:
a kind of courage.

Amazed that air could become so solid,
he mirrored then my other, more daily self:
confused, testing. Despite the holes
I worried about his breathing, tried
to explain with my eyes: experiment.
He longed for a corner, I could tell.
And the horrible clicks when he hopped,
the top of the jar a sky he could count on.
How escape vengeance? Twisting the lid slowly,
the moment electric with messages,
I held the opened mouth at arm's length
until its one word faltered, then sprang.
I dropped the jar and ran for the nearest sidewalk,
hoping to see a mailman, some friend, a dog,
anything normal.

Or sometimes, crouching there, I would huddle
inside myself like the hard dark fruit
of the horse chestnut, imagining spikes.
I would build on that image outward: stem,
the ingenious branches, the leaves sly as tongues,
the firm thigh of the mother trunk, and the black roots
spreading like unnamed side roads on a map.
I would imagine God as a boy the size of myself
finding me here after looking and looking,
his patience as long as the strings of kites,
and as lucky. And knowing that I had found a better
place than the corners of all the kitchens,
he would slide inside the adjoining space
and curl as tight as myself, our secret safe, he
being my only brother.

The years have confused everything,
like an altar boy who thought he knew the response
when he started to open his mouth:
"And I will go to the altar of God—
to God, the joy of my youth." "I will praise
you on the harp, O God my God. Why are you sad,
my soul, and why do you sigh within me?"

In a Boston bus station a black black man
stumbles toward me with his breath and mutters:
"I hungry, I beggin' hard!" And I,
fresh into the real world, blush
at the pock-faced lady across the way.

Significances cower in every corner
and without pause, and I am torn,
and I take you with me, applying your being
like a bandage on the world, that bleeds
and bleeds, my God, anyway.

2.

It is hard, Lord, to live in this world
that cries Be hard, Be soft.
It is hard to live with the beauty of bodies,
the ugliness of bodies, the tactlessness
of mirrors. It is hard
to live with the cricket's ease of song,
the groan of boys in bathrooms,
the grace of a match-flame,
the lovers clutching their sorry remnants,
the suicide falling to the river
like a student exhausting his repertoire
of excuses.

And the waitresses, the sellers of cars,
the believers in statistics:
how their faces amaze me if I look,
and the hands of derelicts that will not remain still,
and the dreams of the misshapen and the ordinary
that linger ahead of them as they walk—
a few inches in front—
like feelers they refuse to trust.

And there are harder truths, facts
that bend all the energy of loving.
Who can measure the ways in which we grow smaller
or hide from our own shallowness,
and what fear can surpass it?
Dailiness, the small tight knots of jealousy,
the desire to be admired by those we admire
that makes us, inevitably, less.

And all the while, time's howl
hacking up the night, the wind
stumbling into the dark rooms of our lives
with its answers, which are wrong—
it is hard. It wakes
the small owl of complaint.

And your words, separate as bones,
that will not seek me out,
that will not gather in the lost trees of houses
where I wait, impatient even with my impatience,
like a husband in bed
whose wife putters in the kitchen,
oblivious of injury, or like a child
waking to a sound or the lack of sound,
the familiar room, the shadows adjustable and safe,
the nightlight's smile, and the fear,
unexplainable, rising, rising.

3.

And this final device,
the self spilling out before we have time
to find a container.

Off Nantucket this year I hear
there are people dying of ticks.
One burrows into the hair of a small girl
unnoticed by doctors whose eyes on the chart
marvel at the graphic destruction. The books
agree she is dying, pages flapping
like loose tongues in a white village.

But there is no child. Only, on the tasteless
palate of pain, a small grain of sweetness,
dissolving.

And I will be dying in Mass General some day,
the nurses fluttering like white handkerchiefs
down the clothesline of a hall, blown only
by my breath, that will not stop calling the names
of her and her who loved me better than all
the poems in the world combined and warned me
when the time came, this would happen.

Or I will be dying in a bed thick with toenails
and hair, the sheets not changed in a month
and the vomit rising like the wrong words to my mouth—
my nose, that never smelled, working finally.

Or I will be dying on a highway in Seattle
struck by a Dodge-driving housewife who will stand
wringing her hands like Viva towels
as the long fingers of my blood
strain toward their last soft shoulder.

If only, Spirit, you could tone down a bit that ending,
one could learn to live with this earth,
the flippant tongues of the sea, the sharp
stars honing their teeth
on the green tree of forever.

4.

All the dead lovers ever, this sea,
are breathing tonight.
Their power is quiet now.
Except for the minor complaint they make
against the shore, turning in their dreams of children,
they make no noise at all.

They would rather have been the limbs of trees,
leaves sprouting from all their fingers.
"What did we ever do but love you?" they ask,
and the rocks shift uneasily,
rubbing their bodies against each other.
"What did we ever do," they murmur, all
the dead lovers ever, this sea
breathing tonight, "but love you?"
and think the question rhetorical.

I think sometimes of those I love—
after a movie maybe, or when the sea
is making these noises even the dead could cherish.
I gather my own death around me,
people it with people I have known,
and move into silence as a stone to water,
glancing back through the thickening grey
to where the ripples widen. The seaweed
sways around me in slow motion,
teaching me to dance: "Even
a stone," it sings, "even a stone."

I am not a stone. I could spin out of myself
songs to startle the fish with, sharp
hooks of songs, and spinners of silvery steel.
Under the waves of my own desire
I cling to what the Spirit says
in the spaces between beginnings,
an always and always of givings and goings
and mirror words.

If lives move somewhere I cannot be
they are no less mine, and they
wake sometimes in the night to a sound
like distant sheet metal shaken,
faint as glass, announcing . . .
nothing they have any need to say.

5.

All things lean toward this, the long fall into silence.
Birds in the air swim—who knows how deep it is?—
we swim, and the future reels us in like fish,
happy to have us. No instruction
the mind takes from the must-be-admired things
will hold or matter:
the glad surfaces greet each other and pass on,
retrievable only as rain is retrievable.

Sometimes, so as not to be outstripped by rain,
words turn to a little meaning.
But the truth is so full of radiant angles,
what cloth will do justice to it,
what sieve not let it run—as a sieve should—
out through the random spaces?
Say there is marvel in stars—or else refuse to say it—
what star will increase or diminish its truculent shine,
its long leave-taking?

And yet the weak eye glances, acknowledging:
it will work, this world, all of a piece,
the small birds, the inveterate singers.
And I have seen flash off the headwaters of LaPush,
mouth-hooked and death hooked, the great Pacific
    salmon,
shaking its useless no in a grey rain,
much the way the bright mind will squander in dreams
its luminous images: terrible, true, forgotten.

Meanwhile, all the lovely earth speaks in its tongues,
the unplanned, unlandscaped places—
Cat's Paw, Hog's Back, Promontory—fields
of Scotch broom, foxglove, wild rose bushes
whose roots ravish hillsides; morning glory.

In the mole's hole the business of life
piles up behind him like a useless accomplishment.
Tears form on the frond's face daily, and daily fall,
more like a clock than any grief we know.

And the trees, with their tall store of years,
how do they manage to spin spirit out of their spirit
continually, surrounded as they are
by this marketplace of a world?
As if it could see a tree, really. As if it could guess
that the wind's moan is the sweet answer
to leaf tongues sliding down bellies of air—
just as, in that slow time when the grass
eases into world space the whole field of green
trembles with pleasure—Lord
God I would clasp you like a lover, would warm
your back in the curve of my chest
and enter you from behind, becoming
your next surprise in a world you only guess at.

But you are the calm brother, whose anger,
always, translates to disappointment.
The bug of love sulks in the jar of my belly,
tired of hopping, sick of its world,
the inevitable lid, the holes you have poked there,
telling me: "Breathe." I have called it "love,"
Lord, for thirty years. It is anger.

6.

Angel, the heart revises, but Anger is closer.
Poised for the throw of vengeance like bronze Poseidon,
you freeze that way and we gaze at you, guessing,
and you let us. If *you*
were the prey toward which the swooping owl
floated like an eyeballed arrow,
tell me you'd sit and think of alternatives.
Rumplestiltskin of the trees, skin
of the trees, trees of some subterranean thought,
the soul's soliloquy bouncing off walls.

The Eskimos have a hundred words for snow
and still the snow won't answer.

"Hundred" is an ugly word, my wife said once.
What did she see in hairy hundreds?
A hundred water buffalo stampeding?
A hundred vultures circling round her head?
A hundred hands in bed with her that night?
"Hundred" is an ugly word, she said,
and having no cause for disbelief I said
Yes to myself, and "Hun-dred! Hun-dred! Hun-dred!"

In my ugliest moments I am most my own,
when wife willow and weed disown me,
I can soar to a depth no love can plumb
save yours alone.
In the soul's skin I wrinkle like leather
and slither a spiny path to the wood.
My anger's a way of going home to the bone,
to the nether stone where moles come from
and the sun's a forever stranger.

"I met this guy today from Cuba to take me to the fiesta,"
says the jolly girl in the green djelabba,
"and I met an Arab who had a djelabba too, and a fez,
and all we could speak in common was Spanish."
She thinks I care, or listen, or am. A door,
I'd open out to a wall; a street, to a canal.

The nun in the grey suit has a strong sense of duty.
My wife had a beauty she'd have saved for her own
if she'd had the choice—which she had,
and didn't. The man in the rusty beard
(who is me) tells baldfaced lies nevertheless
and the lines by his eyes are frowns from the word
"sex."

"Cut it off!"
shouts the clown with the foul mouth (who is me)
but the nun in grey (who is me) grimaces
and flexes her firm convictions,
and the girl (who is me) in the green djelabba
returns, and my wife (who is me) also,
and I writhe in my sleep—the snake!—
and wake to a scream of all my faces.

7.

Last night, again, I had the dream of paper—
scrap paper in high sparse grass, under billboards,
along the sides of railroad tracks—
remnants of messages people were trying to tell us once,
if only Eat Wheaties, or This End Up.

And waking, I thought of the first man
who ever said "Coca-Cola"—whose wife, perhaps,
even as the word came,
was moaning to the stroke of a stranger's fingers
in the back seat of a Chevrolet.

I thought of my mother
writing a note to my teacher, saying:
Gary missed school on Tuesday because he was sick—
winding this further secret of ours,
like a lover's knot, around me.

I thought of the graveyards of cars
and the graveyards of people, and of the difference,
which seems to hinge on neatness, and flowers
that collapse like bad metaphors.

I thought of Jerry Grant and me
perfecting our private whistle,
pooling our strengths against the strangeness of girls,
and losing, and of Thomas Grubham,
the fattest kid in the Cub Scouts,
who could never get the hang of cruelty
no matter how hard
we pumped it into him.

I thought of my grandmother, Nannie,
with her eighty-year harvest of smiles,
coasting toward death confused and lonely,
like a train pulling into heaven
through the worst part of town.

I thought of bricks, in junk heaps,
that will never lie flat against each other,
of windows whose glass has been replaced
by cardboard, or nothing,
of insects, from whom we snatch the one life
as though we were blowing our noses, of coins
dropping neatly into the coin returns of telephones
whose one message is: busy.

And falling asleep again, I dreamt of words,
words with faces that never turn out right,
words that no one has thought of, really,
that might have successfully said: "I love you"
or: "I *want* your child" or
whatever words have to say
to make things live.

8.

Tonight the world reads like a dustjacket blurb
that says I am troubled. Lord,
I am not troubled, exactly.
By the light of a luminous woman
I am seeking the one honest man within:
they all grin, have navels, know how to ape
the boyish innocence.

I think of those children
who collect holy cards; who have a prayer
for everything; who believe if they ask for it long enough
that the wand in the bottom drawer—bought
at the five-and-dime—will turn real magic overnight;
who assume, when it doesn't, that they didn't.
Children who thrive on Lent, that time
when the statues of saints go purple,
each face a hangman's—a time for giving up
not ghosts, but pennies, bubble gum, the movies.

I smile at that, but I have sighed for children
bent in dark confessionals, hushed,
waiting with the frightened rabbits of their sins
that this magician, without benefit of wand,
will make vanish—children who have chosen the better
part, though it *will* be taken from them,
and who sigh in their lovely turn
for me—"fallen away" like the Easter rock,
a part of the background out of the light
of that blinding card that now they see
and now they don't, in their land of celebration
and of tears.

But picture your son pushing at that boulder
with only his human strength, the angel out there
    waiting,
checking his watch, and the third day waning, and the
    world—
the blurb I mentioned earlier—saying: Now,
for the first time ever. . . !

And the prop-changer, how he scurries,
sleight of hand and slighter of mind,
slighter of women. Say what you will, I
have to live with myself daily and know better than
    anyone
the thick debris, how scattered here and there,
and still stumble.

And meantime you play your war games with the sea,
machine-gun up the sky with stars, announcing:
Look at this! When will you grow up, God
my God, and learn that lightning is superfluous?
A few words say besides these flourishes,
this fanfare—as, for instance,
what do I do now, or you,
now that I need you?

9.

I would tell you this in Spanish, if I knew Spanish,
if I knew what word I wanted to say.
La Palabra—to have such a word for *word*!

I would tell you this in some simpler way than words.
Lot's wife, and Eurydice: if a look
can do that, what need for a landslide of nouns?

And yet all things you make
are made with care, and of parts, small
and many. Patience is your first name.
I have watched hummingbirds make feasts out of
    foxglove,
hawks hover, the tips of their wings
reading the wind like Braille, and at night bats
stumble against the dark, pretending.
I have seen the goldfish, seen them in the pond,
their tails white and silk and see-through
all at the same time, and moving all ways
at the same time. I have seen pools so still, so clear,
that peering down from sheer rock
I could read the backs of rainbow trout
once I could track them: they would dart,
stop, start again, as flies in the blue air
sliced squares out of sunlight. I have seen
the marigolds, oblivious of scholars,
spinning their own sunshine: petals, petals,
and, inside, rows and rows inside of rows—
yes
I would be your poem, your words in the order you
    desire—
but I'd like to say it once and then lie down and sleep
without dreaming the dream of paper, the dream of
    words,

I'd like to say it once
and get it over with, to catch my soul
when it's not looking and mold with my hands
the one true word that would break
like a clean sea across silence,
that would hang in the blue air
like the slit left by the wingtip of the hawk
as our eyes stand there waiting for blood
or water or even fire to spill,
that lodges instead in the lung like a foreign body
or as though the moon were a plate
we keep trying to smash on the black floor of the sky.

There are cities, Lord—whole cities—
and streets in those cities, and in those streets
people, and streets in those people
and even in those streets people
passing each other like synonyms for "pain,"
each with its own shade of meaning,
passing from silence to silence, from birth to death,
as though they were changing buses.

And you are the bus driver,
cursing at the people who will not hurry,
cursing and waiting. You are the Christmas papa,
clutching the set of directions that correspond somehow
to our spontaneous muddlings. You are the man
in the jewelry store, who cannot release a watch
without checking it against his own
and turning the stem with a kind of precision
that astounds the common customer.
If you are who are, who are you?

At most I am a space between your words,
and how can a space, leaving, leave a space?

10.

The true voice finds its home, salmon-smart,
or like sperm, which, even missing the mark,
die, I like to imagine, happy.
There is in the self a place like this:
harbors. But a verb.

I return like a child on a swing to the same pair of hands,
to a kind of silence, the kind
that gathers at the mouths of rivers—
the Little Nestucca, its leaning kiss to the sea
at that good moment when the tides equal each other—
the silence of fallen trees in whose rotted stumps
field mice hide from the swooping owl, mice
in whose furry skins ticks will burrow,
in whose tiny bowels the atoms announce:
we come again tomorrow but in new clothes—
raiment of rain, perhaps, wraps of the sun.

But the mind like a light clicks off,
and only your hands can separate
the soft chambers of creation.

Spirit,
your answers lie lost somewhere—no,
not lost, misplaced—or placed, rather, where they belong
but where we have yet to look,
like the notes we find between pages of books
years later and half remember, half forget.

The place we are not does not exist, we think,
and then, going, find that the world thrives
without us: incredible.
Whole families on the klongs of Bangkok,
brushing their teeth in the fetid water,
flagging down vegetable boats, existing, busy.

Who knows what spiked image
you plan to drive into our hearts today,
what happy things wait like familiar coats
on the backs of so many chairs?
It is as if, on our one day off,
we had called in sick, this choosing,
these lives that wait for us—here,
there. Yours, though we call them
ours.

Library of Congress Cataloging in Publication Data

Miranda, Gary.
    Listeners at the breathing place.
    (Princeton series of contemporary poets)
    I.   Title.
PS3563.I69L5   811'.5'4   78-54153
ISBN 0-691-06368-0
ISBN 0-691-01353-5 pbk.